WOODLAND WILDLIFE

White-Tailed Deer

by G. G. Lake

CAPSTONE PRESS
a capstone imprint

Pebble® Plus

Pebble Plus is published by Capstone Press,
1710 Roe Crest Drive, North Mankato, Minnesota 56003
www.mycapstone.com

Library of Congress Cataloging-in-Publication Data
Names: Lake, G. G., author.
Title: White-tailed deer / by G. G. Lake.
Description: North Mankato, Minnesota : Capstone Press, [2017] | Series:
    Pebble plus. Woodland wildlife | Audience: Ages 4–8 | Audience: K to
    grade 3 | Includes bibliographical references and index.
Identifiers: LCCN 2016001763| ISBN 9781515708193 (library binding) | ISBN
    9781515708261 (pbk.) | ISBN 9781515708322 (ebook (pdf))
Subjects: LCSH: White-tailed deer—Juvenile literature.
Classification: LCC QL737.U55 L346 2017 | DDC 599.65/2—dc23
LC record available at http://lccn.loc.gov/2016001763

Editorial Credits
Gena Chester, editor; Juliette Peters, designer;
Wanda Winch, media researcher; Steve Walker, production specialist

Photo Credits
Dreamstime: Framed1, 13; iStockphoto: LarryLynch, 21; Shutterstock: Mike Rogal, 9,
alicedaniel, illustrated forest items, Anna Subbotina, 22–23, AR Pictures, tree bark
design, elina, 24, mythja 1, Pictureguy, 7, Ron Rowan Photography, 5, Stawek, 11 (map),
Sunny Forest, 3, Tom Reichner, cover, 17, Valerie Johnson, 15, Victoria Hillman, 19,
Volodymyr Burdiak, 11 (top)

Note to Parents and Teachers

The Woodland Wildlife set supports national curriculum standards for science related
to life science. This book describes and illustrates white-tailed deer. The images
support early readers in understanding the text. The repetition of words and phrases
helps early readers learn new words. This book also introduces early readers to
subject-specific vocabulary words, which are defined in the Glossary section. Early
readers may need assistance to read some words and to use the Table of Contents,
Glossary, Read More, Internet Sites, Critical Thinking Using the Common Core,
and Index sections of the book.

Printed and bound in China
PO007726LEOF16

Table of Contents

Graceful Runners

A white-tailed deer walks along the edge of the woods. It stops and looks around. Danger! The deer lifts its tail, showing white fur. It runs quickly away.

White-tailed deer have long legs.

Their legs help them run fast.

These deer can run up to

30 miles (50 kilometers) per hour.

Male deer have antlers.
These bones grow on top
of a deer's head. Deer use their
antlers to fight other male deer.

Woodland Homes

White-tailed deer live in North America
and parts of South America.
They usually live in open areas
along the edges of woods.

White-Tailed Deer Range Map

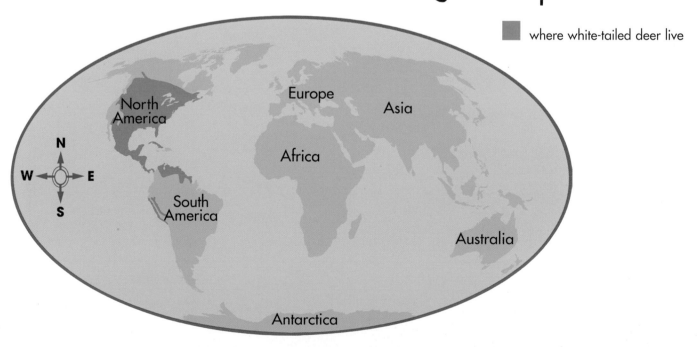

North America

Europe

Asia

Africa

South America

Australia

Antarctica

N
W   E
S

White-tailed deer travel in an area called a home range. They stay in this range their whole lives. They sleep in different areas of their home range. They may rest in tall grass.

13

Forest Food

White-tailed deer eat leaves, flowers, and grass. They will eat almost any type of plant. Deer search their entire home range for food.

Staying Safe

Bears, wolves, and humans hunt white-tailed deer. Deer stay safe by staying quiet. Their coloring keeps them hidden. It blends in with their forest homes.

Fawns

Baby deer are called fawns.
Mothers give birth to two fawns
every spring. Within an hour,
the fawns can walk.

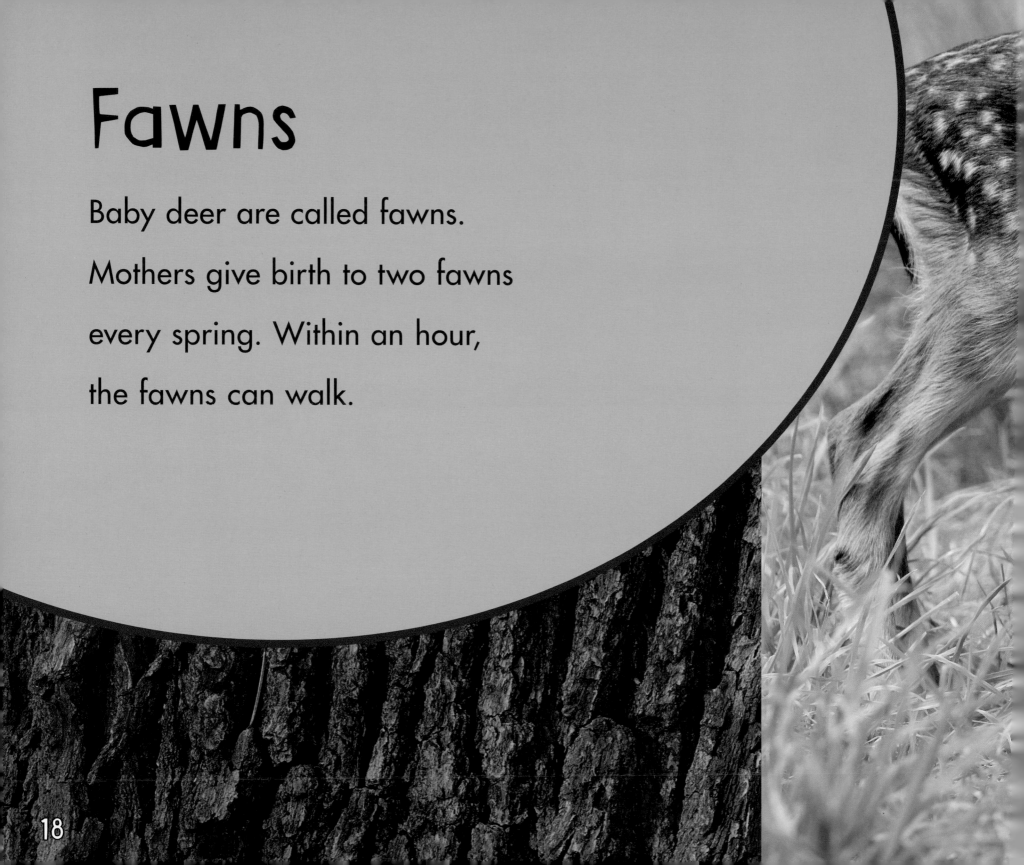

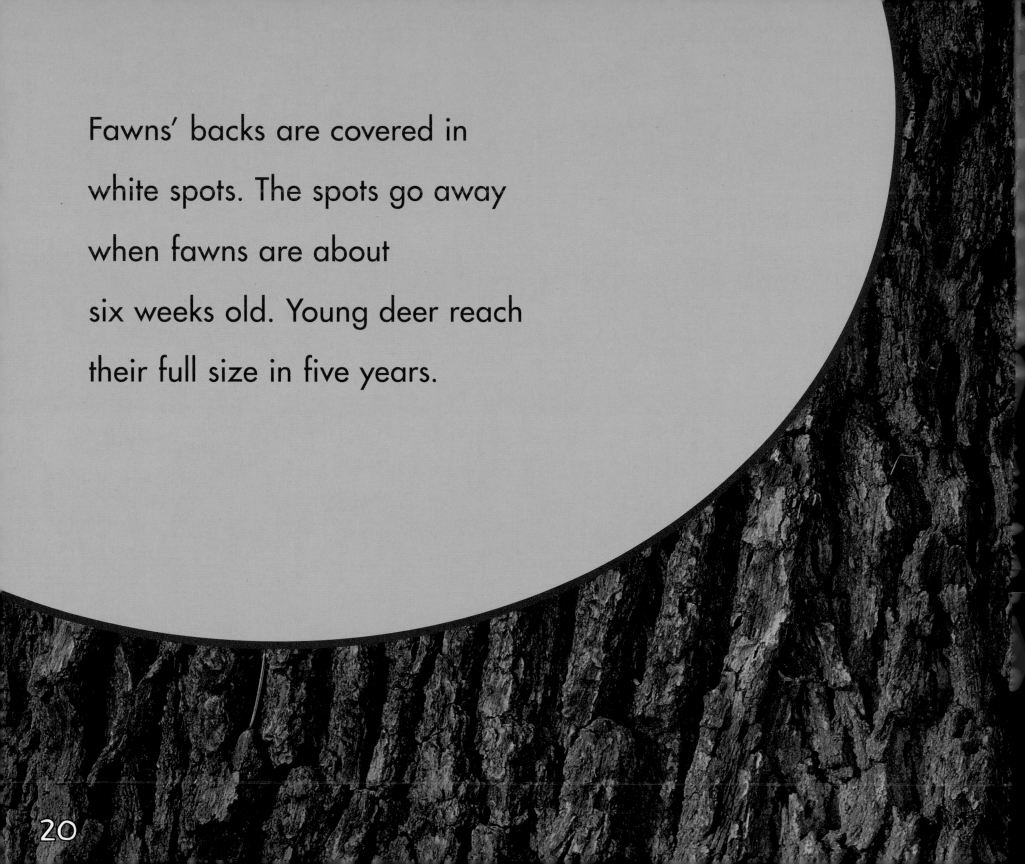

Fawns' backs are covered in white spots. The spots go away when fawns are about six weeks old. Young deer reach their full size in five years.

Glossary

antler—one of the large, branching, and bony growths on a male deer's head

blend—to fit in with the surroundings

fawn—a baby deer

home range—the area in which a deer travels to find food

hunt—to find and catch animals for food

woods—a large area covered with trees and plants; forests are sometimes called woods

Read More

Bowman, Chris. *White-Tailed Deer.* Minneapolis, Minn.:
Bellwether Media, 2015.

Marsico, Katie. *White-Tailed Deer.* Nature's Children.
New York: Children's Press, 2014.

Meryl, Magby. *White-Tailed Deer.* North American Animals.
New York: PowerKids Press, 2014.

Internet Sites

FactHound offers a safe, fun way to find Internet sites
related to this book. All of the sites on FactHound have
been researched by our staff.

Here's all you do:

Visit *www.facthound.com*

Type in this code: 9781515708193

Super-cool stuff!

Check out projects, games and lots more at
www.capstonekids.com

Critical Thinking Using the Common Core

1. What is a home range? (Key Ideas and Details)

2. How long does it take for a fawn to walk? (Key Ideas and Details)

3. Where are white-tailed deer not found? (Craft and Structure)

Index